Grandmothers
are
Forever

Dr. Criswell Freeman

WG
WALNUT GROVE PRESS
NASHVILLE, TN

Grandmothers

are
Forever

Dr. Criswell Freeman

Walnut Grove Press
Nashville, TN 37203

2nd Edition
ISBN 1-58334-140-4

The ideas expressed in this book are not, in all cases, exact quotations, as some have been edited for clarity and brevity. In all cases, the author has attempted to maintain the speaker's original intent. In some cases, material for this book was obtained from secondary sources, primarily print media. While every effort was made to ensure the accuracy of these sources, the accuracy cannot be guaranteed. For additions, deletions, corrections or clarifications in future editions of this text, please write Walnut Grove Press.

Printed in the United States of America
Cover & Page Layout Design by Bart Dawson
Cover Photo: www.comstock.com
1 2 3 4 5 6 7 8 9 10 • 02 03 04 05 06 07 08 09 10

Acknowledgments: The author is indebted to Angela Freeman, Dick and Mary Freeman, Ron Smith, Jim Gallery, and to the creative staff at Walnut Grove Press.

For Virginia Criswell, Marie Freeman,
and Angie Knight

Table of Contents

Introduction

This book pays tribute to grandmothers everywhere. And with good cause. Grandmothers reshape eternity through their influence on future generations. But, this is as it should be because without grandmothers, there would be no future generations to influence.

In my own case, I am continually blessed by the lives of two special women, my own grandmothers: Virginia Criswell and Marie Freeman. My grandmothers helped shape me in ways that I am only now beginning to understand. And, the more I learn about myself, the more I understand the priceless gift of caring, loving grandparents.

So if you happen to be a grandmother, thank you for all you have done and continue to do. And if you happen to be a grandchild sneaking a peak at Grandma's quotation book, remember that grandmothers are forever. And, remember that all you are you owe to your grandmother...in more ways than one.

Chapter 1
Grandmothers Are...

*Grandmother is just
another name for love.*

—

Old-Time Saying

*T*he dictionary defines the word "grandmother" as "the mother of one's father or mother." But thoughtful grandchildren know that the true meaning of the word "grandmother" can never be defined so easily.

A grandmother is usually asked to assume many roles: She is teacher, confidante, babysitter, family historian, spiritual advisor, family counselor and short-order cook. A grandmother is the foundation of the family, often the glue that holds the clan together. She guides her children and grandchildren by serving as role model and advice-giver of last resort.

On the pages that follow, we pay tribute to the women who keep grateful grandchildren thanking their lucky stars for their great grandmothers.

A grandparent is like a wise elder,
        more detached than a parent.

—Richard Walker

Grandparents are our living link to the past.

—George Bush, Sr.

If a family has no grandparent, it possesses no jewel.

—Chinese Proverb

Being a grandmother is above all a learning experience.

—Sheila Kitzinger

Grandmothers are the bearers of tradition.

—*Judith Stevens-Long*

A grandparent is a unique kind of emotionally involved,
part-time parent without pressure.

—*Dr. Fitzhugh Dodson*

I thank God for my grandmother who stood
on the word of God and lived with the spirit
of courage and grace.

—*Maya Angelou*

Her children arise up, and call her blessed.

—*Proverbs 31:28 KJV*

We learn to be grandmothers, just as
we learn to be mothers.

—Sheila Kitzinger

Grandparents are the family watchdogs.

—Lillian E. Troll

If you would civilize a man, begin with
his grandmother.

—Victor Hugo

Grandparents have a special kind of love.

—Eda LeShan

Almost all grandmothers agree that
grandparenting is easier than parenting.

—*Judith Stevens-Long*

Becoming a grandmother brings the satisfaction
of giving and receiving love, sometimes more freely
and more generously than ever before.

—*Shelia Kitzinger*

The connection between grandparents and
grandchild is natural and second
in emotional power only to the bond
between parent and child.

—*Arthur Kornhaber*

A grandmother is a person who has time.

—Anonymous child's definition

Grandparents are more patient, more tolerant,
more aware of little changes
in their grandchild.

—Nancy Reagan

Grandma was a first-aid station who restored
us to health by her amazing faith.

—Lillian Smith

Grandmothers Last A Lifetime... And Beyond

Lin Yutang observed, "Of all the rights of women, the greatest is to be a mother." And, if motherhood is the world's greatest privilege, surely grand-motherhood is among the world's greatest delights.

The role of grandmother can be a joyful experience indeed, but wise grandmothers do much more than simply play with their grandchildren or baby-sit them. Thoughtful grandmothers serve as enduring, lifelong role models.

Through words and deeds, a grandmother's influence extends beyond time and space, weaving itself as an unbroken thread through future generations. In truth, a grandmother's impact upon her family lasts a lifetime...and beyond.

Happiness is being

a grandmother.

—

Jan Stoop and Betty Southard

Chapter 2
Grandchildren Are...

Perfect love does not

sometimes come until

the first grandchild.

—

Welsh Proverb

*G*randchildren are bountiful blessings to the grandparents who, without direct parental control, can usually enjoy their offspring at a safe distance. Herein, we explore the joys of observing, teaching and loving the children's children. May they live happily ever after.

Posterity is the patriotic name for grandchildren.

—*Art Linkletter*

Children are our immortality—in them we
see the story of our life written in a fairer hand.

—*Alfred North Whitehead*

Here's my advice: Make sure your children
and grandchildren know you love them.

—*Barbara Bush*

Love is caught, not taught.

—*Frank Laubach*

Your children are your investment.
Your grandchildren are your dividends.

—*Anonymous*

A child is the greatest poem ever known.

—*Christopher Morley*

Children must be valued as
our most priceless possession.

—*James Dobson*

Every child born into the world is a new thought
of God, an ever-fresh and radiant possibility.

—*Kate Douglas Wiggin*

A baby is God's opinion that life should go on.

—*Carl Sandburg*

Better many children than many riches.

—*Vietnamese Proverb*

When a grandchild is born, all relationships
in the family shift and change.
—*Sheila Kitzinger*

When you have a grandchild, you have two children.
—*Yiddish Saying*

Give a little love to a child and you get a great deal back.
—*John Ruskin*

Every child who comes into the world presents
a new possibility for lifting the destiny
of the human race.
—*Anna B. Mow*

Every child's relationship with a close and
loving grandparent is unique.

—*Arthur Kornhaber*

There was never a child so lovely but
his mother was glad to get him asleep.

—*Ralph Waldo Emerson*

Blessed be childhood, which brings down
something of heaven into the midst
of our rough earthliness.

—*Henri Frédéric Amiel*

Wherever children are, there is the golden age.

—*Novalis*

A sweet child is the sweetest thing in nature.

—*Charles Lamb*

In the eyes of its grandmother, every beetle is a gazelle.

—*African Proverb*

Your sons weren't made to like you.
    That's what grandchildren are for.

—*Jane Smiley*

Grandchildren Are...

A grandchild is a bundle of love wrapped in possibilities. No wonder that every grandbaby is the light of grandma's eyes.

Henry Ward Beecher proclaimed, "Children are the hands by which we take hold of heaven." A grandmother, by taking firm hold of her grandchild's hand, creates a little piece of heaven here on earth.

The secret of life is to skip having children and go directly to grandchildren.

—

Mell Lazarus

Chapter 3
Love

A grandmother's love

is like no other love

in the world.

—

Old-Time Saying

A grandmother's love is a wonderful thing for grandmoms and grandkids alike. A grandchild who has been lucky enough to feel the secure love of a caring grandparent will never forget that experience. And, a grandparent who feels the touch of an adoring grandchild is changed forever.

Love is the currency by which life is denominated, a currency that is multiplied as it is spent. And, as we all know, when it comes to this currency of love, grandmothers are biggest of the big-time spenders. Thank goodness!

Love doesn't make the world go round.
Love is what makes the ride worthwhile.

—*Franklin P. Jones*

There is a net of love by which
you can catch souls.

—*Mother Teresa*

Love is the river of life in the world.

—*Henry Ward Beecher*

There is only one terminal dignity—love.

—*Helen Hayes*

The closest friends I have made all through life
    have been people who also grew up close to a loved
        and loving grandfather and grandmother.

—Margaret Mead

Love doesn't sit there like a stone, it has to be made
    like bread; remade all the time; made new.

—Ursula K. LeGuin

Love stretches your heart and makes you big inside.

—Margaret Walker

Love is multiplication.

—Marjory Stoneman Douglas

Love is the master key which opens the gates
of happiness.

—Oliver Wendell Holmes, Sr.

Let your grandchildren know, through words and deeds,
that the bond of affection which attaches
the two of you to one another can never
be broken.

—Arthur Kornhaber

A child's hand in yours—what tenderness it arouses,
    what power it conjures. You are instantly
    the very touchstone of wisdom and strength.

—*Marjorie Holmes*

To love children is to love God.

—*Roy Rogers*

Accustom yourself continually to make many
    acts of love, for they enkindle and melt the soul.

—*St. Teresa of Avila*

Confidence is the best proof of love.

—Maria Edgeworth

There is nothing so loyal as love.

—Alice Cary

If one wishes to know love, one must live love.

—Leo Buscaglia

To love is to receive a glimpse of heaven.

—Karen Sunde

You can give without loving,
 but you cannot love without giving.
                              —*Amy Charmichael*

Love does not dominate; it cultivates.
                              —*Goethe*

Love is shown by deeds, not words.
                              —*Philippine Proverb*

To love abundantly is to live abundantly, and
  to love forever is to live forever.

—*Anonymous*

When we come right down to it,
  the secret to having it all is loving it all.

—*Dr. Joyce Brothers*

Love is the only true freedom. It lets us cast
  off our false exteriors and be our real selves.

—*Susan Polis Schutz*

A Grandmother's Love

Grandmothers understand the power of love, and they share that message with the entire family. A grandmother shares her love through words and—more importantly—through deeds. The beneficiaries of that love are forever blessed.

A grandmother's love becomes her permanent legacy, her timeless gift to the family. It is a gift to her children, to her grandchildren, and to subsequent generations.

You will find, as you look back upon your life, that the moments when you have really lived are the moments when you have done things in the spirit of love.

—

Henry Drummond

Chapter 4

Home

Home is the place where

the great are small and

the small are great.

—

Robert Savage

*I*t has been said that "home is where the heart is." It must be added that a grandchild's *second* home is where grandmother is. Fortunate kids build lifelong memories around the fun and games at Grandmother's.

In this chapter, we examine some of the essential elements of a happy, functional home. And, we learn what savvy grandmoms have known all the while: A real home is any building built upon a foundation of love.

It takes a heap o' lovin' in a house to make it a home.

—*Edgar A. Guest*

A house is not a home.

—*Polly Adler*

A house is no home unless it contains food
and fire for the mind as well as for the body.

—*Margaret Fuller*

Home—that blessed word which opens
to the human heart the most perfect glimpse
of Heaven.

—*Lydia M. Child*

Houses are like the hearts of men, I think,
 They must have life within. They must have fires
  and friends and kin, love for the day and night,
 children in strong, young laps. Then they have life.

—*Lenora Speyer*

Everyone has, I think, in some quiet corner
 of his mind, an ideal home waiting to become a reality.

—*Paige Rense*

I have been very happy with my homes,
  but homes are no more than the people
   who live in them.

—*Nancy Reagan*

Home is not a way station:
>It is the profession of faith in life.
>>*—Sol Chaneles*

It takes a hundred men to make an
>encampment but one woman to make a home.
>>*—Robert Ingersoll*

The woman who creates and sustains a home
>is a creator second only to God.
>>*—Helen Hunt Jackson*

Make two homes for thyself: one actual home
and another spiritual home which thou art
to carry with thee always.

—*St. Catherine of Siena*

Home ought to be our clearinghouse,
the place from which we go forth lessoned
and disciplined, and ready for life.

—*Kathleen Norris*

Home is where you learn values.
It's the responsibility of the family.

—*Melba Moore*

Home is where

the heart is.

—

Pliny the Elder

Home Is...

Home is not simply a place; it is a state of mind, built as much with love as with brick and mortar. The size of a house is relatively unimportant; the collective size of the hearts that dwell inside is all-important.

What is a home? It is a place where we are protected and loved. It is a place where we are free to be ourselves. It is a place where we celebrate our victories and find comfort in our defeats. Home is the place where we gather together with loved ones and share this wonderful gift called life. In other words, home is just about the very best place on earth.

Home wasn't built

in a day.

—

Jane Ace

Chapter 5
Family

*The strength of a nation drives
from the integrity of the home.*

—

Confucius

*G*randmothers, having raised the children who raise the children, possess special insights into family life. So when it comes to matters of house and home, wise kids and grandkids seek the advice of their clan's most experienced mother.

The observations, tips, and common-sense advice in this chapter are intended for families everywhere. And, if these words sound suspiciously like those uttered by grandmother, so be it. After all, grandmother knows best.

The family—that dear octopus from whose tentacles
we never quite escape, nor, in our inmost hearts,
ever quite wish to.

—*Dodie Smith*

Family life is the source of the greatest
human happiness.

—*Robert J. Gavinghurst*

Call it a clan, call it a network, call it a tribe,
call it a family. Whatever you call it,
whoever you are, you need one.

—*Jane Howard*

Healthy families are our greatest national resource.

—*Dolores Curran*

A family is a school of duties...founded on love.

—*Felix Adler*

A family is a place where principles are hammered
and honed on the anvil of everyday living.

—*Charles Swindoll*

The happiest moments of my life have been
spent in the bosom of my family.

—*Thomas Jefferson*

Family is the we of me.

—*Carson McCullers*

When the whole family is together,
the soul is in place.

—Russian Proverb

If I were starting my family over again,
I would give first priority to my wife
and children, not to my work.

—Richard Halverson

Marriage is a covered dish.

—Swiss Proverb

A happy family is but an earlier heaven.

—Sir John Bowring

Most men need more love than they deserve.

—Marie von Ebner-Eschenbach

A successful marriage requires falling in love
many times, always with the same person.

—*Mignon McLaughlin*

Marriage is not just spiritual communion and
passionate embraces; marriage is also three meals a day,
sharing the workload, and remembering
to carry out the trash.

—*Dr. Joyce Brothers*

No kingdom divided can stand—
neither can a household.

—*Christine de Pisan*

A successful marriage is not a gift;
it is an achievement.

—*Ann Landers*

When a marriage works, nothing on earth
can take its place.

—Helen Gahagan Douglas

Better a hundred enemies outside the house
than one inside.

—Arabian Proverb

What we learn within the family are
the most unforgettable lessons that
our lives will ever teach us.

—Maggie Scarf

Loving Our Families

When Mother Teresa received her Nobel Prize, she was asked, "What can we do to promote world peace?" She replied, "Go home and love your family." That's powerful advice for parents and grandparents alike.

No duty is more important than that of loving and caring for our families. When we give of our time, our energy, and our love, the next generation reaps rich rewards...and so do we.

*A bonus of being a grandmother
is being with babies and toddlers —
and rediscovering the delights of play.*

—

Shelia Kitzinger

Chapter 6
The Younger
Generation

Every generation revolts against its parents and makes friends with its grandparents.

—

Lewis Mumford

*E*very generation is the same, only different. But sometimes, parents are simply too close to the firing line to realize that their kids are not so unlike themselves. Mom and dad may panic, fearing that their children are irresponsible, strange, or worse. What's needed is perspective. And who better to provide this perspective than grandmother? After all, she's a card-carrying member of the generation that has "seen it all" and lived to tell about it.

Grandparents understand that the more kids change, the more they remain the same. So parents take notice: Your children have the same hopes and dreams that you had at their age. But as for the hairstyles and clothing, well that's an entirely different matter.

Youth is wholly experimental.

—*Robert Louis Stevenson*

Youth, even in its sorrows, always has
a brillancy of its own.

—*Victor Hugo*

Beautiful is youth because it never comes again.

—*George Jean Nathan*

When you're young, the silliest notions seem
the greatest achievements.

—*Pearl Bailey*

Youth is the time of life when one believes
he is immortal.

—William Hazlitt

Young folks will have their own way.

—Martha Washington

Children are all foreigners.

—Ralph Waldo Emerson

Children are like clocks...they must be allowed to run.

—James Dobson

The life of children, as much as that
of intemperate men, is wholly governed
by their desires.

—Aristotle

Adolescence can be a time of turmoil and
turbulence. Rebellion against authority
and convention is to be expected.

—Haim Ginott

There is no sinner like a young saint.

—Aphra Behn

No man knows he is young while he is young.

—*Lord Chesterfield*

The excesses of our youths are drafts upon
our old age, payable with interest
about thirty years after date.

—*Charles Caleb Colton*

Childhood is never troubled with foresight.

—*Fanny Burney*

Youth is the time to go flashing from one end
of the world to the other, both in mind
and body.

—Robert Louis Stevenson

Every age has its own follies.

—American Saying

Like its politicians and its wars,
society has the teenagers it deserves.

—J. B. Priestly

A child becomes an adult when he realizes
that he has a right not only to be right
but to be wrong.

—Thomas Szasz

With teenagers and their music in the house,
      I can only say one thing, "Thank God for a
            hearing impediment."

—*Liz Carpenter*

My interest in young people is in rumpling
      their brains as you might rumple
            a good head of hair.

—*Robert Frost*

In general my children refuse to eat anything
      that hasn't danced on TV.

—*Erma Bombeck*

A cynical young person is almost the saddest
    sight to see because it means that he or she has
    gone from knowing to believing in nothing.

                                              —*Maya Angelou*

You know children are growing up when
    they start asking questions that have answers.

                                        — *John J. Plomp*

It's a shame that we cannot have all the wisdom
    one is ever to possess in the beginning.

                                    —*Zora Neale Hurston*

Nature makes boys and girls lovely to look
    upon so they can be tolerated until they
    acquire some sense.

                                  —*William Lyon Phelps*

It is amazing how quickly the kids learn to drive a car,
yet are unable to understand the lawn mower,
snow blower or vacuum cleaner.

—*Ben Bergor*

There are three ways to get something:
do it yourself, employ someone,
or forbid your children to do it.

—*Monta Crane*

Youth is a fever of the mind.

—*La Rochefoucauld*

Teen is a four-letter word.

—*Popular Saying*

Don't panic even during the storms
of adolescence. Better times are ahead.

—James Dobson

Don't limit a child to your own learning
for he was born in another time.

—Rabbinic Saying

Children need love, especially when they
do not deserve it.

—Harold S. Hulbert

We cannot always build the future for our youth,
but we can build our youth for the future.

—Franklin D. Roosevelt

Children have more need of models than of critics.

—*Joseph Joubert*

What children learn at home is what they will
take with them when they are grown.

—*Chuck Christensen*

Parents, grandparents, and children each have
something to give each other.

—*Fitzhugh Dodson*

When you listen to your children, you are paying
them a compliment. By listening, you increase their
feelings of self-respect and self-worth.

—*Dean and Grace Merrill*

*It's hard to know where
one generation ends and
the other begins. But
it's somewhere around
nine o'clock at night.*

—

Charles Ruffing

Chapter 7
Life

Life is what we make it.

Always has been;

always will be.

—

Grandma Moses

*L*ife is a great mystery to us all, grandmothers excluded. Somehow, somewhere, grandmothers just figured things out. Thankfully, they are always willing to share their hard-earned knowledge—if the younger generation is willing to slow down long enough to listen.

This chapter contains grandmotherly advice about life. Kids, grandkids, great-grandkids, even casual bystanders, please take notice!

It is more important to live the life one wishes
    to live, and to go down with it if necessary,
    quite contentedly, than live more profitably
    but less happily.

          —*Marjorie Kinnan Rawlings*

Two things everybody's got to do for themselves:
    They've got to trust God and they've got to
    find out about living for themselves.

          —*Zora Neale Hurston*

Yesterday is a canceled check, and tomorrow's
    a promissory note. But today is cash,
    ready for us to spend in living.

          —*Barbara Johnson*

Every day is a messenger of God.

—Russian Proverb

Time is the stuff of which life is made.

—Benjamin Franklin

Life is a succession of moments,
　　　　to live each one is to succeed.

—Corita Kent

When you were born, you cried and the world rejoiced!
Live your life in such a manner that
when you die, the world cries and you rejoice.

—Old Indian Saying

Write it on your heart that every day is
the best day of the year.

—*Ralph Waldo Emerson*

Don't anticipate the happiness of tomorrow.
Discover it today.

—*Ella Wheeler Wilcox*

I could never be content to simply look on.
Life was meant to be lived. We must never,
for any reason, turn our backs on life.

—*Eleanor Roosevelt*

Life is a party; you join after it's started and
you leave before it's finished.

—*Elsa Maxwell*

Life is right now.

—*Barbara Bush*

To live is to fight, to suffer and to love.

—*Elizabeth Leseur*

It is important to stay close enough to the pulse
of life to feel its rhythm, to be comforted by
its steadiness, to know that life is vital,
and one's own minute living a torn fragment
of the larger cloth.

—*Marjorie Kinnan Rawlings*

God has a plan for all of us, but He expects us
to do our share of the work.

—*Minnie Pearl*

The greater part of our happiness depends
      on our disposition and not our circumstances.
                              —*Martha Washington*

It's not the load that breaks you down,
               it's the way you carry it.
                              —*Lena Horne*

It has begun to occur to me that life is a stage
               I am going through.
                            —*Ellen Goodman*

Surely the consolation prize of old age
      is finding out how few things are worth
               worrying over.
                            —*Dorothy Dix*

Life is partly what me make it and partly
        what is made by the friends we choose.

—*Chinese Proverb*

The fingers of God touch your life
        when you touch a friend.

—*Mary Dawn Hughes*

The best mirror is a trusted, old friend.

—*Sephardic Saying*

Associate with those who help you believe in yourself.

—*Brooks Robinson*

It is great to have friends when one is young,
  but indeed it is still more so when you are getting old.
When we are young, friends are, like everything else,
  a matter of course. In the old days we know
    what it means to have them.

—*Edvard Grieg*

The making of friends, who are real friends,
  is the best token we have of success in life.

—*Edward Everett Hale*

Old friends are best unless you catch
  a new one fit to make an old one out of.

—*Sarah Orne Jewett*

Remorse is the poison of life.

—*Charlotte Brontë*

Every hour is a stranger to you—
until you live it.

—*Zora Neale Hurston*

Mistakes are the portals of discovery.

—*James Joyce*

Never fear shadows. They simply mean there's
a light shining somewhere.

—*Ruth E. Renkel*

The life that doesn't have a sense
of responsibility to something broader
than one's self is not much of a life.

—*Gail Sheehy*

Life begets life. Energy creates energy.
It is by spending oneself that one becomes rich.

—*Sarah Bernhardt*

We can learn so much from vital older
women who live their passions
with purpose and direction.

—*Gail Sheehy*

Love the moment and the energy of the
moment will be spread beyond all boundaries.

—*Corita Kent*

The spiritual eyesight improves
as the physical eyesight declines.

—*Plato*

All the flowers of all the tomorrows are
in the seeds of today.

—*Anne Outland*

What we are is God's gift to us.
What we become is our gift to God.

—*Eleanor Powell*

Most things have an escape clause,
　　　　　but children are forever.

—Lewis Grizzard

Children are the messages we will send to
　　　　　a time we will never see.

—Neil Postman

It's never too late—in fiction or in life—to revise.

—Nancy Thayer

We are here to help one another along life's journey.

—William Bennett

The Gift of Life

Having given the gift of life, who better to explain it than grandmothers? And, make no mistake about it: life is indeed a gift—courtesy of our mothers and grandmothers—a gift that should be treasured and used to the fullest.

Grandmothers view life with the wisdom that is gained through years of experience. They realize that life can be—and should be—a work of art. And, savvy grandmoms help their kids make each day—and each life—a masterpiece.

Each day comes bearing its own gifts.
Untie the ribbons.

—

Ruth Ann Schabacker

Chapter 8
Memories

God gave us memories that we might have roses in December.

—

James M. Barrie

*I*t has been said that memory is the thing we forget with. But, some memories are simply too priceless to lose. Happy remembrances of days gone by compose the fabric of life; they make us who we are. Other memories, those that breed bitterness or regret, are best discarded with vigor and haste.

The lessons in this chapter teach us that a retentive memory can be a blessing or a curse, depending upon how it is used. So all of us are advised to do what savvy grandmothers do: we should practice the art of memory management, because we can never be fully contented until we remember to forget the things that don't need remembering. And vice versa.

No man can know where he is going
   unless he knows exactly where he's been.

—Maya Angelou

Look at the past. Don't hide from it.
   It will not catch you if you don't repeat it.

—Pearl Bailey

Lord, keep my memory green.

—Charles Dickens

Remember childhood visions.

—Mary McCleod Bethune

Memory moderates prosperity, decreases
adversity, controls youth and delights old age.

—*Lactantius*

To be able to enjoy one's past is to live twice.

—*Martial*

Relationships with other people have
made my life incredibly rich.

—*Barbara Bush*

The little present must not be allowed wholly
to elbow the great past out of our view.

—*Andrew Lang*

Praising what is lost makes the remembrance dear.

—William Shakespeare

Time…our youth…it never really goes,
    does it? It is all held in our minds.

—Helen Hooven Santmyer

Memory is a painter, it paints pictures of the past.

—Grandma Moses

A grandparent's memories, those tales of times past,
    that seasoned view of the world—these are
    priceless gifts which the grandparent alone can
    offer their grandchildren.

—Arthur Kornhaber

Old friends are the great blessing of one's
    later years. They have a memory of the same events
        and have the same mode of thinking.

—Horace Walpole

There's no friend like someone who has
        known you since you were five.

—Anne Stevenson

It is my friends who have made the story of my life.

—Helen Keller

The companions of our childhood always possess
        a certain power over our minds.

—Mary Shelley

Women and elephants never forget.

—*Dorothy Parker*

A retentive memory may be a good thing,
    but the ability to forget is the true token
        of greatness.

—*Elbert Hubbard*

Make it a rule of life never to regret and
    never to look back. Regret is an appalling waste
        of energy; you can't build on it;
        it is only good for wallowing in.

—*Katherine Mansfield*

The things we remember best are those better forgotten.

—*Baltasar Gracián*

How we remember, what we remember, and why we
remember form the most personal map
of our individuality.

—*Christina Baldwin*

Memory is the diary we all carry within us.

—*Mary H. Waldrip*

Friends fill the memory with sweet things.

—*Martha Washington*

In memory each of us is an artist; each of us creates.

—*Patricia Hampt*

Some folks never exaggerate—they just remember big.

—*Audrey Snead*

*Grandmothers
are full of memories.*

—

Margaret Walker

Lessons in Faith

Grandmothers, having seen it all more than once, understand the power of faith. As Grandmoms know all too well, faith is the foundation upon which great lives are built. Faith is a gift we give ourselves that pays rich dividends in good times or bad.

Wise grandmothers teach the power of faith by word and by example. When they do, fortunate grandchildren learn that faith protects...and perfect faith protects perfectly.

Grandparents are the living link to the family's past.

—

Arthur Kornhaber

Chapter 9
Raising Grandkids

*The secret of dealing
successfully with a child
is not to be its parent.*

—

Mell Lazarus

*M*ost grandparents help raise their grandchildren at arm's length. In such cases, a little distance can be a very healthy thing. Because parents' parents are usually somewhat removed from the daily grind of child-rearing, they can offer counsel with a certain degree of objectivity. Such level-headed advice is badly needed since parental objectivity, as we all know, is a commodity much rarer than gold.

In this chapter, we examine ways that grandparents make a difference in the lives of their grandkids...a big difference.

Can grandmas make a difference in the lives
of their grandchildren?
Absolutely, but it takes energy and love.

—*Jan Stoop and Betty Southard*

For baby-sitting grandparents, love and exhaustion go
hand in hand.

—*Eda LeShan*

The role of teacher is one of the most important
for any grandparent.

—*Arthur Kornhaber*

Helping our children is often the best way
 to help our grandchildren.

—Eda LeShan

Grandmothers especially are frequently
 called on to be a mother's personal
 support system.

—Arthur Kornhaber

Grandmothers can model love
 in a very special way.

—Jan Stoop and Betty Southard

A good-listener grandma tries to hear
 the feeling behind the words that are spoken.

—Jan Stoop and Betty Southard

If grandparents want to have a meaningful and
constructive role, they must learn that becoming
a grandparent is *not* having
a second chance at parenthood.

—*Eda LeShan*

Never tell your children how to raise their children.

—*Fitzhugh Dodson*

An important goal for grandparents
is not to compete with parents.

—*Eda LeShan*

Very rarely will you make a mistake by keeping quiet
about something concerning your grandchildren.

—*Fitzhugh Dodson*

A child's education should begin at least
    a hundred years before he is born.

—Oliver Wendell Holmes, Sr.

A great gift to one's child is knowledge.

—Christine de Pisan

Education is the jewel casting brilliance into the future.

—Mari Evans

The potential possibilities of any child are
    the most intriguing and stimulating in all creation.

—Ray L Wilbur

Inspire youngsters to develop the talent
            they possess.

—Augusta Savage

Those who are lifting the world upward
            and onward are those who encourage
                more than criticize.

—Elisabeth Harrison

Teaching is the art of assisting discovery.

—Mark Van Doren

Children have to educated, but they also
            have to be left to educate themselves.

—Abbé Dimnet

Learning in childhood is like engraving on a rock.

—*Arabian Proverb*

As the twig is bent, so the tree grows.

—*Virgil*

Trees bend only when young.

—*Jewish Saying*

What children learn at home is what they
will take with them when they are grown.

—*Chuck Christensen*

Praise your children in public,
correct them in private.

—*Old Saying*

The hearts of small children are delicate organs.

—*Carson McCullers*

Children need love, especially when they
do not deserve it.

—*Harold S. Hulbert*

Kind words can be short and easy to speak,
but their echoes are truly endless.

—*Mother Teresa*

Listen! Encourage. Say something.
 Do something. Be yourself. Love.

—Dale Turner

The school will teach children how to read, but the
 environment of the home must teach them
 what to read. The school can teach them
 how to think, but the home must teach
 them what to believe.

—Charles A. Wells

Education is not filling a pail, but lighting a fire.

—William Butler Yeats

His heritage to his children wasn't words or possessions,
but an unspoken treasure, the treasure
of his example as a man and a father.

—*Will Rogers, Jr.*

Children have never been very good at
listening to their elders, but they have
never failed to imitate them.

—*James Baldwin*

Children are very much aware of integrity;
when they see it they know it, though they
wouldn't know the word.

—*Eudora Welty*

He who lives well is the best teacher.

—*Cervantes*

Education is life, not books.

—*African Proverb*

Our children observe us all day long, at our best
and at our worst. Much of what they learn comes
simply from living with us and observing us.

—*Shirley Suderman*

To teach good behavior one wisely understands
that young people must play and laugh.

—*Christine de Pisan*

The most deprived children are those who have
to do nothing in order to get what they want.

—Sydney J. Harris

Do not handicap your children
by making their lives easy.

—Lazarus Long

At every step the child should be allowed to meet
the real experiences of life; the thorns should
never be plucked from his roses.

—Ellen Key

Never help a child with a task at which
he feels he can succeed.

—Maria Montessori

You must teach your children to dream
with their eyes open.

—Harry Edwards

The goal of disciplining our children is to encourage
their growth as respectful, responsible,
self-disciplined individuals.

—Don H. Highlander

Loving a child doesn't mean giving in to all
his whims; to love him is to bring out the best
in him, to teach him to love what is difficult.

—Nadia Boulanger

Remember, when they have a tantrum,
don't have one of your own.

—Judith Kurisansky

Good grandparenting begins early,
    long before the birth of the first grandchild.
                        —Arthur Kornhaber

When women talk about their own
    grandmothers, the thing they value most was the
        grandmother's willingness to listen.
                        —Sheila Kitzinger

When you are dealing with a child,
    keep your wits about you and sit on the floor.
                        —Austin O'Malley

Don't take up someone's time talking about
    the smartness of your grandchildren. He wants to talk
        about the smartness of his.
                        —E. W. Howe

Take responsibility for the future of society
        by raising responsible children.

—Kaye Gibson

Never argue with a child or a fool.

—American Saying

Wherever children are learning,
        there dwells the Divine Presence.

—Old Saying

Was there ever a grandparent tired after
    a day of minding noisy youngsters, who hasn't felt the
        Lord knew what he was doing when
        he gave little children to young people?

—Joe E. Wells

*L*ittle children have big ears.

—

American Saying

Chapter 10
Forever Young

As soon as you feel too old

to do a thing, do it.

—

Margaret Deland

*Y*outh is transitory, but a youthful spirit need never grow old. On the pages that follow, we consider a checklist of proven ways to retain or regain that youthful spirit.

The ideas in this chapter compose the roadmap to a bubbling fountain of youth that exists within all of us. It is a fountain of our own construction; how we drink depends upon how we think.

Youth has no age.

—Pablo Picasso

Life before 50 is nothing but a warm-up.

—Advertisement for AARP

Though it sounds absurd, it is true to say
　　I felt younger at sixty than I felt at twenty.

—Ellen Glasgow

My interest is in the future because
　　I'm going to spend the rest of my life there.

—Charles F. Kettering

Grandparenting is a marvelous opportunity
     to keep alive, alert, growing and giving.
                                        —*Fitzhugh Dodson*

The secret to longevity is keeping active all the time.
                                        —*Milton Berle*

Keeping busy is the answer.
                              —*Marjory Stoneman Douglas*
                              On her 100th birthday

Painting is not important. The important thing
     is keeping busy.
                                        —*Grandma Moses*

We turn not older with years, but newer every day.

—*Emily Dickinson*

Youth is a gift of nature; age is a work of art.

—*Anonymous*

Her grandmother, as she gets older,
            is not fading but rather becoming
                more concentrated.

—*Paulette Bates Alden*

Age is all imagination. Ignore years and
            they will ignore you.

—*Ella Wheeler Wilcox*

Aging is a timeless ascent. As power diminishes,
we grow toward the light.

—*May Sarton*

The most fulfilled older people maintain
a state of mind that, rather than clinging
fearfully to the past, accepts change
and encourages growth.

—*Connie Goldman and Richard Mahler*

I never feel age. If you have creative work,
you don't have age or time.

—*Louise Nevelson*

Live your life and forget your age.

—*Frank Bering*

To me, old age is always fifteen years older than I am.

—*Bernard Baruch*

If wrinkles must be written upon our brows,
let them not be written upon the heart.
The spirit should never grow old.

—*James A. Garfield*

A man is not old until regrets take the place
of his dreams.

—*John Barrymore*

Whatever wrinkles I got, I enjoyed getting them.

—*Ava Gardner*

I feel more at peace with myself than
        when I was an ambitious young woman.

—Jessica Tandy

You can't help getting older, but you don't have to get old.

—George Burns

Age is a case of mind over matter.
        If you don't mind, it doesn't matter.

—Jack Benny

It's not how old you are, but how you are old.

—Marie Dressler

Nobody ought to be too old to improve.

—*Anna Letitia Barbauld*

You don't grow old; when you cease to grow, you are old.

—*Charles Judson Herrick*

If we don't change, we don't grow.
If we don't grow, we are not really living.

—*Gail Sheehy*

Only in growth, reform and change,
paradoxically enough, is true security found.

—*Anne Morrow Lindbergh*

Change is the constant, the signal for rebirth,
the egg of the phoenix.

—*Christina Baldwin*

There are very few things you can do to defy
the aging process. Keeping your hopes alive
is definitely one of them.

—*Stanley H. Cath*

Of all the things you wear, your expression
is the most important.

—*Janet Lane*

Wrinkles should merely indicate
where smiles have been.

—*Mark Twain*

Aging slowly does not mean doing battle
with the passing years.
It means enjoying them to the hilt.

—Myron Brenton

Activity does not wear out the human machine
and spirit...inactivity does.

—Garson Kanin

The excitement of learning separates you
from old age. As long as you're learning,
you're not old.

—Rosalyn S. Yalow

Age is bothersome only when you stop
to coddle it.

—Maurice Chevalier

Anyone who keeps the ability to see beauty
never grows old.

—*Franz Kafka*

All that is good in man lies in youthful
feeling and mature thought.

—*Joseph Joubert*

You are only young once, and if you work
it right, once is enough.

—*Joe E. Lewis*

There's the beauty of age, more profound,
more complete. It forms a fine patina that
only life and living can impart.

—*Karen Westerberg Reyes*

The first forty years of life give us the text:
    the next thirty supply the commentary.

—Schopenhauer

In youth we learn. In age we understand.

—Marie Ebner-Eschenbach

The evening of life brings with it its lamp.

—Joseph Joubert

All that I know I learned after I was thirty.

—Georges Clemenceau

Middle age is when you don't have
    to have fun to enjoy yourself.

—Franklin P. Jones

You stay young as long as you can learn,
acquire new habits and suffer contradictions.

—*Marie von Ebner-Eschenbach*

The key to change...is to let go of fear.

—*Rosanne Cash*

The person who has lived the most is not
the one with the most years but the one
with the richest experiences.

—*Jean Jacques Rousseau*

Look up and not down; look forward and not back;
look out and not in; and lend a hand.

—*Edward Everett Hale*

Do not deprive me of my age.
I have earned it.

—

May Sarton

Attitude

A grandmother's attitude is contagious. If she is optimistic and upbeat, the family will tend to be likewise. But, if grandmother falls prey to pessimism and doubt, the family suffers right along with her.

Wise grandmoms understand the power of positive thinking. These special women share a message of encouragement and hope with those around them, especially with their children and grandchildren. And savvy grandmothers, as they spread their happiness and optimism, can't help getting a little on themselves.

You can't turn back the clock.
But you can wind it up again.

—

Bonnie Prudden

Chapter 11
Grandmother's
Advice

The one important thing I've learned over the years is the difference between taking one's work seriously and taking one's self seriously. The first is imperative, and the second is disastrous.

—

Margaret Fontey

*W*ho knows more than Grandmother? Nobody! And if you don't believe it, just ask her. So we conclude with a potpourri of wisdom that would make any grandmother proud.

We carry the seeds of happiness with us
wherever we go.

—*Martha Washington*

Always keep that happy attitude.
Pretend that you are holding
a beautiful fragrant bouquet.

—*Candice M. Pope*

Live each day as it comes, and don't borrow
trouble by worrying about tomorrow.

—*Dorothy Dix*

Happiness walks on busy feet.

—*Kitte Turmell*

Without faith nothing is possible. With it,
nothing is impossible.

—*Mary McLeod Bethune*

In spite of everything I still believe that people
are really good at heart. I simply can't build up
my hopes on a foundation consisting
of confusion, misery and death.

—*Anne Frank*

The way I see it, if you want the rainbow,
you've got to put up with the rain.

—*Dolly Parton*

One thing that doesn't abide by majority rule
is a person's conscience.

—*Harper Lee*

If you listen to your conscience, it will serve
you as no other friend you'll ever know.

—*Loretta Young*

Service is the rent you pay for room on this earth.

—*Shirley Chisholm*

I don't want to get to the end of my life and find
that I just lived the length of it. I want to have
lived the width of it as well.

—*Diane Ackerman*

Service to a just cause rewards the worker
with more real happiness and satisfaction
than any other venture of life.

—*Carrie Chapman Catt*

When you cease to contribute, you begin to die.

—*Eleanor Roosevelt*

Believe that your tender, loving thoughts
and wishes for good have power to help the struggling
souls of earth rise higher.

—*Ella Wheeler Wilcox*

This is happiness; to be dissolved
into something complete and great.

—*Willa Cather*

The best and most beautiful things in the world
cannot be seen or even touched. They must be felt
with the human heart.

—Helen Keller

It is only possible to live happily-ever-after
on a day-to-day basis.

—Margaret Bonano

Happiness is a matter of one's most ordinary
everyday mode of consciousness, being busy
and lively and unconcerned with self.

—Iris Murdoch

Keep what is worth keeping and with the
breath of kindness blow the rest away.

—Dinah Maria Murlock Craik

There is no good reason why we should not
    develop and change until the last day we live.
                                        —*Karen Horney*

I tell everybody to travel and not get married too soon.
                                        —*Moms Mabley*

The search for instant gratification is harmful.
                                        —*Shirley Ann Grau*

The best time to make friends is before you need them.
                                        —*Ethel Barrymore*

If I'd realized how much fun grandchildren were,
I'd have had them first!

—*Faith Myers*

If you don't want your children to hear what
you're saying, pretend you're talking to them.

—*E. C. McKenzie*

I have found the best way to give advice
to your children is to find out what they
want and then advise them to do it.

—*Harry S. Truman*

The best things you can give your children,
      next to good habits, are good memories.

—*Sydney J. Harris*

Good manners will often take people where
      neither money nor education will take them.

—*Fanny Jackson Coppin*

The end is nothing. The road is all.

—*Willa Cather*

Make beauty a familiar guest.

—*Mary Howitt*

A woman is like a tea bag. You never know
how strong she is until she gets into hot water.

—*Eleanor Roosevelt*

If you think you can, you can.
If you think you can't, you're right.

—*Mary Kay Ash*

My grandmother used to say a day is wasted
if you don't fall over at least once with laughter.

—*Luci Swindoll*

Treat the world well. It was not given to you
by your parents but lent to you by your children.

—*Ida B. Wells*

Each day, look for a kernel of excitement.

—Barbara Johnson

I never really look for things. I accept whatever
God throws my way. Whichever way God
turns my feet, I go.

—Pearl Bailey

Earth's crammed with heaven.

—Elizabeth Barrett Browning

Faith can put a candle in the darkest night.

—Margaret Sangster

Dignity is like a perfume; those who use it
are scarcely conscious of it.

—*Queen Christina of Sweden*

Charm is simply this: the golden rule, good manners,
good grooming, good humor, good sense,
good habits, and a good outlook.

—*Loretta Young*

Take the back roads instead of the highways.

—*Minnie Pearl*

When young people ask me how I made it,
I say, "It's absolutely hard work.
Nobody's gonna wave a magic wand."

—*Loretta Lynn*

About the Author

Criswell Freeman is a Doctor of Clinical Psychology living in Nashville, Tennessee. He is the author of *When Life Throws You a Curveball, Hit It* and numerous books in the Wisdom Series published by WALNUT GROVE PRESS.

His Wisdom Books chronicle memorable quotations in an easy-to-read style. The series provides many inspiring, thoughtful and humorous messages from entertainers, athletes, scientists, politicians, clerics, writers and renegades. Combining his passion for quotations with extensive training in psychology, Freeman revisits timeless themes such as perseverance, courage, love, forgiveness and faith.

Dr. Freeman is also the host of *Wisdom Made in America*, a nationally syndicated radio program.